# NTHOLOGY OF SACRED SONG

CELEBRATED ARIAS SELECTED FROM

ORATORIOS

BY OLD AND MODERN COMPOSERS

EDITED BY MAX SPICKER

VOL. 1. SOPRANO
2. ALTO
3. TENOR
4. BASS

Ed. 523

G. SCHIRMER, Inc.

Distributed by
HAL LEONARD PUBLISHING CORPORATION
Winona MN 55987 Milwaukee WI 53213

# Anthology of Sacred Song

## Alto

### Index of Oratorios

# Anthology of Sacred Song

## Alto

### Index of Oratorios—*Continued*

# Anthology of Sacred Song

## Alto

### Index of Authors

# Anthology of Sacred Song

## Alto

### Index of Authors—*Continued*

# Anthology of Sacred Song

# Christmas Oratorio.

## Aria.

J. S. BACH.

fec-tion, Pre-pare thy-self, Zi-on, with ten-der af-
fec-tion the pur-est, the fair-est, this day to-re-ceive, pre-pare thy-self,
Zi-on, with ten-der af-fec-tion the pur-est, the fair-est, this day to-re-
ceive, the fairest, the pur-est, pre-pare thy-self, Zi-on,
with ten-der af-fection, pre-pare thy-self,
mf
f
p
cresc.
p cantabile
tr

cresc.
Zi - on, with ten-der af - fec-tion, the pur-est, the fair-est, this day to re-ceive.
cresc.
f
tr
tr
tr
Fine.
p espress.
Thou must meet Him with a heart with love o'er - flow - ing,
p
cresc.
with a heart with love o'er - flow - ing, haste then, with ardor the Bride-groom to

mf poco agitato
wel-come, haste then, haste then, with ar-dor the Bride - - -
poco agitato
groom to wel-come, haste then, with ar-dor the Bridegroom to welcome.
tr
f
tr
p espress.
Thou must
p più tranquillo
meet Him with a heart with love o'er-flow - - - -
cresc.
- - ing, haste then, with ardor the Bride-groom to welcome.
allarg.
tr
col canto



D. C. al Fine.

# Christmas Oratorio.

## Aria.

J. S. BACH.

thy re - pose, slum-ber, be - lov - ed, and take thy re - pose,
p
Soon wilt thou wak-en, our joy and sal - va - tion, Slum - ber, be - lov-ed, and
take thy re - pose,
mf
Soon wilt thou wak-en, our joy and salva-tion.
f

dolce
Slum - ber, be - lov - ed, and take — thy re - pose,
slum - ber, be -
pp
lov - ed, and take — thy re - pose,
Soon wilt thou waken, our joy — and sal -
cresc.
tr
p
va - tion, — soon wilt thou wak - en, our joy and sal-va - tion, wak - en,
cresc.
wak - en, soon — wilt thou wak - en, soon wak - en, our
tr
cresc.
tr
joy — and salva - tion.
cresc.
f

rall.
Fine.
p espress.
cresc.
O! may thy breast find glad-ness and rest In our heart-felt ex-ul-
ta - tion, in our heart-felt ex-ul-ta-
- tion. O! may thy breast find glad - ness and
espr.
p
f

rest In our heart-felt ex-ul - ta - - tion, O! may thy

breast find glad - ness and rest In our heart-felt ex-ul - ta -

- - tion, O! may thy breast find glad-ness and rest

*tr* *f* *p* *f* *p*

*mf*

In our heart-felt ex - ul - ta - - - -

*r.h.*

*cresc.* *rall.* *tr*

- - - - - - tion.

*rall.*

*D. C. al Fine.*

# St. Cecilia.

## Arioso.

Sir J. BENEDICT.

smorz.
rall.
pray'r and praise, up - on Thy_ ser - vants' pray'r and_ praise.
dim.
pp
colla voce
a tempo
p con espress.
O, let us Thy pro - tec - tion share,_ O
cresc.
let us Thy pro - tec - tion share,_ And give us grace the
p un poco meno mosso
pp
poco cresc.
worst to bear, and give us grace the worst to bear, If

più cresc.
poco string.
cru - el men cut short our days, if cru - el men cut
r.h.
poco string.
mf
p calando
short our days, if cru - el men cut short our days. O
mf
p
poco a poco rit.
give us grace the worst to bear, O give us grace the worst, the
poco a poco rit.
pp
Tempo I.
p
worst to bear. Fa - ther, whose bless - ing we en -
pp
treat, Look down-ward from Thy mer - cy-seat Up - on Thy

cresc. - - - assai

ser - vants' pray'r and praise, Look down-ward from Thy mer - cy -

ff dim.

seat Up - on Thy ser - vants' pray'r, Thy ser -

pp

vants' pray'r and praise, O Fa - ther, look

rit. cresc. dim.

down - ward up - on Thy ser - vants' pray'r.

perdendosi

# St. Peter.

## Aria.

Sir J. BENEDICT.

poco rit.
p a tempo
ness shalt Thou, shalt Thou be es - tab - lish - ed; O Thou af -
a tempo
poco rit.
flict-ed, and toss-ed with tempest, O Thou af - flict-ed, and toss-ed with
tempest, af flict-ed and not com - fort - ed: Thou shalt be
mf
p
far from op - pression, for Thou shalt not fear,
p
mf
pp
p
Thou shalt be far from op - pres - sion, for Thou shalt not fear,
cresc.
f
cresc.
f

dim.
p
and from terror,
for it shall not come
mf
near Thee. No weapon a - gainst Thee shall pros-per, and ev - e - ry tongue
mf
p
cresc.
in judg - ment Thou shalt con - demm.
cresc.
f
dim.
p con
O
sentimento
Thou af - flict-ed, and toss-ed with tem-pest, O Thou af -
cresc.
flict-ed, and toss - ed with tem-pest, and toss-ed with tempest, af-
cresc.

mf
flict-ed and not com - fort - ed: Be -
cresc.
hold, in right - eous - ness shalt Thou be es -
dim.
cresc.
tab - lish - ed, Thou shalt be
cresc.
f
rall. molto
far from op - pres - sion, for Thou
col canto
p tranquillo
shalt not fear, Thou shalt not fear.
p

# The Woman of Samaria.

## Aria.

Larghetto espressivo.

S. BENNETT.

mine up - ris - - ing,
Thou un - der -
p
p tranquillo
stand - est my thoughts long be - fore,
sf
long be - fore, my thoughts,
sf
pp
long be - fore. O Lord, Thou hast
p
pp tranquillo
colla parte
pp
search - ed me out, and known me;
pp

pp
for lo! there is not a word,
pp stacc.
sf
not a word in my tongue,
sf
p
but Thou
p
knowest it al-to-geth-er.
espress.
p
tranquillo
O Lord, thou hast search-ed me out, and
calando
pp tranquillo
known me. Thou know-est my down-

cresc.
sit - ting, Thou know - est my down - sit - ting
sf
poco cresc.
sf
p
and mine up - ris - - ing, and mine up -
p
ris- - ing; Thou know - est it
p
sempre pp
p
rall.
al - to - geth - er, Thou know - est it
rall.
pp
al - to - geth - - er.
pp
colla parte

The Fall of Jerusalem.
Recitative and Aria.
English version by
Dr. Th. Baker.
M. BLUMNER.
Allegro.
f
Recit.
My warning heed, all
ye who love our Lord!
a tempo
My
fa-ther, E-le-a-zar, is con-tend-ing with fran-tic hordes, ris'n in wild re-
bel-lion. Dis-loy-al zeal-ots, head-ed by Jo-han-nes, son of Le-vi of
Gis-kala, have sur-round-ed the tem-ple's court-yard that my fa-ther guards. And

Si - me - on, son of Jo - rash, lead - ing hosts of plun - der-ing I - du -
manains on to save the cit-y, rag-es there un-hinder'd. Three-fold fratricide dis-
ff agitato
honors Zion, while e'er the land resounds with tread of marching Romans,
mf
cresc.
Andante.
fp
f
who, as fain t'a-venge their fail-ure, are pressing hard on us from ev'ry side. Now
p
fear in-spires the heart of all the na-tion to seek for hid-den trai - tors.

mf
Tempo I.
On a sud-den, thro' ev-'ry by-way flies the fa-tal
f
p
word: The low-ly band of Na-za-renes, they are the pois'nous serpent on the breast of
Zi-on.
a tempo
f
Then flee with no de-
lay from out the town!
a tempo
f
p più tran-
The Lord a-
quillo e con calore
bide with you! Be ev-'ry heart up-lift-ed by the pow-er of His
pp

Spir - it! On Him, our Guide and Helper, I re-ly, who ne'er in need or sorrow shall for-
Andante tranquillo.
sake me!
dolce
Aria.
Andante tranquillo, ma non lento.
p
Thine, O Saviour, Thine is love un-end-ing, Thou art e'er my
pp
Guard-ian and my Guide, Thou art e'er my Guard - ian and my
cresc.
dim.
Guide, Thou sus-tain-est them that faint - ing lan-guish, bread of life
p

poco cresc.
to all the hun - gry giv - est, Thou sus - tain - est them that
calando
faint - ing lan - guish, bread of life to all, bread of life
rit.
a tempo
to all the hun - gry giv - est.
rit.
p
mf
p con calore
Thine, O Sav - iour, Thine is love un - end - ing,
dim.
pp
cresc.
Thou art e'er my Guard - ian and my Guide, Thou in
p
cresc.
p

dim.
me and I in Thee, O Lord, Then grace is my portion ev - er - more,
pp
Thou in me and I in
cresc.
Thee, O Lord, then grace is my portion,
p
then grace is my portion, my portion ev - er - more,
p calando
then grace is my portion,
ritard.
then grace is my portion ev - er - more!
pp
mf
p

# Eli.

## The Morning Prayer.

M. COSTA.

dolce e tranquillo
Lord, from my bed again I rise, To
sempre sotto voce
offer up the sacrifice Of praise and
pray'r to Thee, the sacrifice Of praise and
pray'r to Thee.
p
I laid me down to
sleep at night,
mf
I trusted in Thine arm of might;
cresc.
f
Thine
mf

con anima
mf
cresc.
arm pro-tect-ed me, Thine arm pro-tect-ed me, pro - tect -
dim.
- ed me.
8
mf
p
Up -
hold Thy ser - vant through the day, Di - rect my steps in
de -
p
cresc.
wis - dom's way, Let me not turn a - side, let me not turn a -
p
poco riten.
p a tempo
side, not turn a - side. Let me not walk where
col canto
p

cresc.
scorn-ers walk, And sin - ful men pro-fane - ly talk;
cresc.
Still be my God, still be my God, my God and
dim.
guide, my God and guide, still
be my God and guide!
rall.
a tempo
p a tempo
pp

# Eli.

## Recitative and Evening Prayer.

M. COSTA.

they that dwell in Thy house; for a day in Thy courts is bet-ter than a
thousand. I had ra-ther be a door-keep-er in the house of my
God, than to dwell in the tents of wick - ed-ness.
a tempo
cresc.
decresc.
pp
a tempo colla voce
cresc.
The Evening Prayer.
Andantino. (♪=96)
This night I lift my heart to Thee, Whose dwell-ing is in heaven a-
bove; O, deign to hear and an-swer me, My Fa - ther- God of love! Art
ten.
pp
p
cresc.

poco cresc.
Thou not, Lord, in ev - 'ry place? Is there a thing be - neath Thy
care? Though An - gels on - ly see Thy face, Yet Thou, O Lord, art
cresc.
ev - 'ry - where, yet Thou, O Lord, art ev - 'ry - where. O
cresc.
p
give Thine An - gels charge to keep Their wings spread o - ver me this
p
cresc.
cresc.
night; Let them de - fend me, let them de - fend me let me sleep,
con calore

cresc.
let me sleep Till dark - ness, till dark - ness melts in light!
cresc.
p
pp po-
dolce
Bless the Lord, my soul; O, bless the Lord;
co a poco con sordino e più tranquillo
dolce e cantabile
And all that is with - in me,
p
bless His ho - ly name! Bless the Lord, O
pp
pp
perdendosi
bless His ho - ly name!

# Ruth.

## Aria.

F. H. COWEN.

dim.
frame; He re - membereth, He re - mem - ber-eth that we are
dim.
dust. My soul long - eth, yea, e-ven faint eth for the
mf
Poco agitato
p
p
courts of the Lord, my soul long - eth, yea, e - ven
mf
p
cresc.
faint - eth for the courts of the Lord; My heart
mf
mf
and my flesh, my heart and my flesh cry out, cry out

p
for the liv - - ing God, my heart and my flesh cry
p
marcato
cresc.
out for the liv - - ing God.
dim.
pp
dim. e rit.
a tempo
p espress.
Like as a fa - ther
rit.
p a tempo
cantabile
pi - ti-eth his chil-dren, so the Lord pi - ti-eth
them that fear Him,
cresc.
like as a fa - ther
cresc.

f
pi - ti-eth his chil - dren, so the Lord
dim. p dim. p
pi - ti - eth them that fear Him, so the
pp Ped. p molto rall. molto rall.
Lord, the Lord, the Lord pi - ti-eth
p rall. colla voce
them, pi - ti-eth them that fear
a tempo pp rall.
Him.

# St. Ludmilla.

**Recitative and Aria.**

A. DVOŘÁK.

Meno mosso, quasi Tempo I.
will I go with thee,
dim.
no, no, no farther will I go with thee, no,
Aria.
Lento.
sotto voce
no, no!
Thy leading would I
had not followed, nor come to this dread-ful spot, thy lead-ing
dim.
would I had not followed, nor come to this dread-ful spot!
cresc.

ff
p
mf
Think, from the time yon a-ged man With-in thy
p
dwell - - ing first ap - peared,
fz
f
Tor - - ment and pain thy soul has
p
f
known, Nor hast thou e'er had peace and
mf
dim.
p

dolce
com - - - fort. The might - y power which his
dim. pp p dolce
teach ing wields, Which from his words like rushing rain is pouring. Has bowed thy
dim. p
cresc.
will, and o - ver - mas - tered thee, And driv-en thee forth from thy
f pp
home! How great has he made thy en - durance!
cresc. pp
How changed thy ways, de - sires, and thoughts! How
f mf dim. p pp

dolce
firm thy frame, so weak a - fore-time!
pp
pp
Yea, I feel that all thy life till now has been
dolce
pp
dolce
trif-ling, and whol - ly vain, I feel that all thy
p
dim.
pp
life till now has been trifling, and whol-ly vain.
f
f
ff
dim.
pp

# Christmas Eve.

## Aria.

NIELS W. GADE.

dolce
Long - - de - sir'd sal - va - tion
p
Comes to bless man - kind;
fz
dolce
Our God's lov - ing -
p
kind - ness,
Yours it is to find.
pp
Lo, the night of
f
p
e - - - - - - vil Soon will pass a -
dim.
sf

p
dim.
way, soon will pass a - way;
pp
con anima
Full and free re - demp - - - tion
f
pp
p
Brings a bright - er day, free re - demp - -
- - tion, Full and free re - demp - - -
riten.
tion Brings a bright - er day.
dim.
riten.

# Christmas Eve.

## Aria.

NIELS W. GADE.

dim.
ing, I read dis - tress and
wrath; I hear the tramp of na -
tions, I hear the tramp of na - tions,
De - struc -
p dim.
- tion round their path.
rit.

Andante con moto.
p
dolce
con anima
pp
But now a cheer - ful morn - ing O'er -
spreads the wea - ry earth, Once more is Hope up -

spring - - - ing, To greet the
Sav - - iour's birth; But now a cheer - ful
morn - - ing O'er spreads the wea - ry earth, Once
more is Hope up - spring - ing, To greet the
Sav - - - iour's birth.
cresc.
f
pp
p
f rall.
rall. col canto

# The Holy City.

**Aria.**

A. R. GAUL.

cresc.
Più mosso. (♩=88)
pard, pre - par'd for them that love Him.
cresc.
mf
mf con
For
anima
He hath pre - par'd for them a cit - y, whose
f
f
build - er and Mak - er is God, He hath pre -
par'd, pre - par'd for them a cit - y, whose

Tempo I.
rall.
p
build-er and Mak - er is God. Eye hath not seen,
rall.
p
hath not seen the things pre-pard for them that love Him.
Più mosso.
mf
p
There re - main - eth, there-fore, a rest for the
cresc.
p
p
peo-ple, the peo-ple of God; there-fore, fear, there-fore,
cresc.
p
Ped.
*
cresc.
fear, lest an - y come short of it, there-fore,

fear, there-fore, fear, lest an-y come short of
dim.
rit.
Tempo I.
it, lest an-y come short, come short of it. Eye hath not
seen, ear hath not heard, nei-ther have en-ter'd
in to the heart of man the things which God hath pre-
espress.
cresc.
rall.
par'd, pre-par'd for them that love Him.
pp

# Ruth.

## Recitative and Aria.

A. R. GAUL.

eyes Up - on Thy ser - - vant here,
And grant me strength thro' life's brief length My woes, my
cresc.
earth - ly woes to bear.
rall.
a tempo
dolce
p
It hath seem'd
well, Al - might-y God,
p
That I should chas - ten'd
be,
But O, I would not stay the rod,
cresc.

cresc.
mf con anima
For all is known, is known to Thee! O
cresc.
mf
gra - cious Lord, cast down Thine eyes Up - on Thy ser - -
cresc.
vant here, And grant me strength thro' life's brief
length My woes, my earth - ly woes to bear.
p
rall.
a tempo
espress.
Ped.

p
If by the way I faint and fall,
rall.
a tempo
Of burdens sore complain,
p
Depart me not, but strength allot,
That I may rise, may
rall.
rise again!
a tempo
p
And when my life on earth is
dolce
rall.
o'er,
Have mercy, Lord, on me,

And let me dwell for ev - er - more With Thee, in
Ped. * Ped. *
mf
Par - a - dise with Thee! If by the
mf
dim.
way I faint and fall, Of burdens sore com -
p
dim.
plain, De - sert me not, but strength al - lot,
cresc.
mf
rall.
That I may rise, may rise a - gain.
mf
rall.
p

# The Ten Virgins.

## Aria.

cresc.
Be Thou so, be so un-to the end, Lead us, lead thou us in-to all
cresc.
l.h.
rall.
truth, our Mak-er, our Mak-er, our Sav-iour, our Friend!
rall.
a tempo
p
Then, tho' we walk through the val-ley of the sha - dow of death, we will
p
fear_ no e-vil, for Thou art with us; Thy rod and Thy staff, they

pp
p
mf
com - fort us, they comfort us, they com-fort us, they com-fort us, they
pp
p
mf
rall.
a tempo
p espress.
com - fort us. Thou art the guide of our youth;
a tempo
rall.
p cantabile
mf
Lead, lead thou us on day and night, Make our path clear,
cresc. - - sostenuto
clear as Thy truth, clear as Thy truth and Thy light.
cresc. - - sostenuto
col canto

# Athalia.

## Recitative and Aria.

G. F. HÄNDEL.

p
O Lord,
pp
oh Lord, whom_we a - dore, whom we a -
dore, whom we a - dore! Shall Ju - dah rise no more, shall
mf
Ju - dah rise no more? Can this be Thy de-cree, can this be Thy de-cree?
Oh Lord, can this be Thy de - cree?

mf
Oh
con anima
Lord, whom we a - dore! Shall Ju-dah rise no more, no
mf
more, no more, no more? shall Ju-dah rise no
more? no more? Oh Lord, can this be Thy de-

cree? Oh Lord, shall Ju-dah rise no
more? Can this be Thy de - cree, can this be Thy de-
cree? Oh Lord, can this be Thy de-
Adagio.
cree, can this be thy de-cree?
col canto
Tempo I.

# Deborah.

## Recitative and Aria.

G. F. HÄNDEL.

mf con spirito ben marcato
In the battle, fame pursuing,
p
mf
mf
in the battle, fame pursuing,
tr
p
We'll with slaughter float the plains, we'll with slaugh -
cresc.
- ter

float
mp ben marcato
the plains, we'll with slaugh - - - - - - - - - - - - - - ter float the plains.
p
mf energico
In the bat-tle,
f
p
fame pur - su-ing, We'll with slaughter float the plains,

(,)
we'll with slaugh - - - - - - - - - - - - - - - - - - - ter,
p
sempre col canto
p
mf
we'll with slaugh-ter float the plains, float the plains.
mf
In the bat - tle,
fame pur - su - ing, We'll with slaugh - ter float the
tr

molto cresc.
plains, well with slaugh - - - - - - - - - -
molto cresc.
Adagio.
- - - - - - - ter, we'll with slaugh-ter float the
plains.
Tempo I.
tr
tr
mf
cresc.
f allargando
tr
Fine.

p
And our ty - rants, low in ru - in,
p
p
Soon shall wear,
cresc.
soon shall wear their cap - tives' chains.
p
cresc.
f agitato
And our ty - rants, low in ru - in, low in ru - in, Soon shall
f
mf
p
p
wear their cap-tives' chains, soon shall wear, soon shall
cresc.
mf
p
poco allarg.
wear their cap - tives' chains.
Tempo I.
col canto
f
D.S. al Fine.

# Hercules.

## Aria.

Allegro ma non troppo. (♪= 84) G. F. HÄNDEL.

the moments of de-light, waft the moments of de-light,
the mo-ments of de-light.
f
p
The smil-ing hours, a
joy-ful train, On silk-en pin-ions waft a-gain, on
leggiero
poco cresc.
silk-en pin-ions waft a-gain The moments of de-
leggiero

*mf*

light, the moments of de - light, the mo - ments of de - light, waft, *p* waft a - gain, waft, *p* waft a - gain the moments of de - light, the mo - ments of de - light.

Adagio. *f* *mf*

Tempo I. *f* *giocoso*

Fine. *p*

Re - turning

pleasures ban-ish woe,
f
p
As ebb-ing streams re-cruit-ed flow, And day succeeds to
p
night. Re-turn-ing plea-sures ban-ish woe, As ebb-ing
streams re-cruit-ed flow, And day suc-ceeds to night,
più lento
and day suc-ceeds to-night, and day suc-ceeds to night.
più lento
f
Da Capo al Fine.

# Israel in Egypt.

## Aria.

G. F. HÄNDEL.

-tain of Thine in-her-it-ance, in the place, oh
p dolce
Lord, which Thou hast made, which Thou hast made
p
p
r.h.
for Thee to dwell in, for Thee to dwell in, to dwell
p
p
cresc.
cresc.
in,
f

p tranquillo
in the sanc - tu - a - - ry, oh
dim.
p
Lord,
p
which Thy hands have e - stab -
mp
tr
tr
p
cresc.
- - - - - lish - ed,
cresc.
f
p tranquillo sempre
in the sanc - - - tu -
p

a - - - - - - ry which Thy
p
p dolce
mp
p
handshave e - stab - - - - - - lish - ed, which Thyhandshave
p più lento
p più lento
— e-stab - lish - ed.
a tempo
mp
mf
dim.

# Joshua.

## Recitative and Aria.

G. F. HÄNDEL.

cresc. dolce

and his sparkling eye Bespeak a he - ro, or an an-gel nigh!

**Aria.**

Largo. (♩ = 72)

un poco p

f marcato

ten.

ten.

p

dolce ed

Aw - ful,

espress.

pleas - ing be - ing, say, If from heav'n thou wing'st thy

dolce

way? if from heav'n thou wing'st thy way? Deign to let thy ser-vant know,

dolce
f
If a friend? or pow'r-ful foe? or pow'rful
p
f marcato
p
cresc.
foe, or pow'r-ful foe,
cresc.
f
p
— or pow'r-ful foe? Aw-ful,
f marcato
pleasing be-ing, say, Deign to let thy ser-vant know,
p
mf
If from heav'n thou wing'st thy way? if from heav'n thou wing'st thy
p

p
p
way? Deign to let thy ser-vant know, If a friend,
p
p
dolce
f
or pow'r-ful foe?
marcato
or pow'r-ful foe,
f marcato
mf
cresc.
f
or pow'r-ful
cresc.
f
espress.
p
foe? Deign to let thy ser-vant know, If a
tr
tr
p
p
rall
cresc.
friend, if a friend, or pow'r-ful foe?
col canto
f

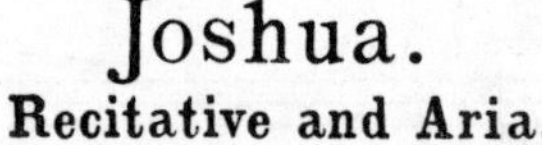

# Joshua.

## Recitative and Aria.

G. F. HÄNDEL.

**Recit.**

*mf*

Now give the ar-my breath, let war a-while Smooth his rough front, and wear a cheer-ful smile. The in-ter-val, if Ach-sah but ap-prove, I'll con-se-crate to vir-tue and to love.

**Aria.**

Tempo di Gavotta.

*mf*

*ben marc.*

*f*

*tr*

*mf ben marcato*

He - roes, when with glo - ry— burn - ing, All their toil with plea - sure bear,

*f*

*mf*

And be - lieve, to love re - turn - ing, Lau - rel - wreaths be - neath their care.

*f*

*mf*

He - roes, when with glo - ry

*p*

burn - ing, All their toil with plea - sure bear, And be - lieve, to love re - turn - ing,

*tr*

cresc.
to love re - turn - ing, Lau - rel - wreaths be - neath their care.
tr
f
p espress.
He - roes,
p
when with glo - ry burn - ing, All their toil with plea - sure bear, And be -
lieve, to love re - turn - ing, Lau - rel - wreaths be - neath their
care,
f
And be - lieve, to love re -

turn-ing, Lau-rel-wreaths be-neath their care, be-neath their
care, And be-lieve, to love re-turn-ing, Lau-rel-
cresc.
wreaths, lau-rel-wreaths be-neath their care.
f
Fine.

mf con spirito
mf
War to har-dy deeds in-vites, war to har-dy deeds in-vites, Love the dan-ger well re-quites, love the danger well re-quites, love the danger well re-quites,
cresc.
p
f
love the dan - - - - ger well re-quites. War to har-dy deeds in - vites,
cresc.
f ben marc.
mf
p dolce
Love the dan-ger well re -

f
quites, War to har - dy deeds in — vites,
Adagio.
con espress.
Tempo I.
Love the dan - ger well — re - quites.
p
f
mf con
Heroes,
spirito
when with glo - ry burn-ing, All their toil with pleasure bear, And be - lieve, to love re -
p
cresc.
turn-ing, Laurel-wreaths beneath their care, lau - rel-wreaths be-neath their care.
cresc.
f
Dal Segno al Fine.

# Judas Maccabaeus.

Aria.

G. F. HÄNDEL.

nize ___ the Feast of _ Lights. Fa-

-ther of Heav'n! from Thy e-ter-nal_throne Look with an_

*con calore*

eye of blessing down; While we pre-pare, ___

_ with ho-ly rites, To so-lemnize ___ the Feast of Lights, the Feast of _

*cresc.*

Lights, to so-lem-nize ___ the Feast of Lights,

*p* *mf* *p* *mf*

un poco allargando
While we prepare, with ho - ly rites, To so - lem - nize the Feast of Lights.
a tempo
p
col canto
mf
And thus our
grate - ful hearts employ;
mf con spirito
And in Thy praise
This altar raise,
cresc.
p
molto cresc.
With ca - rols of tri - um - phant joy,
mf
This al - tar raise, With ca - rols of tri - um - phant
f
joy,
with carols of tri - um - phant joy.
p a piacere
Fa - ther of Heav'n,

a tempo
p
from Thy e-ter-nal throne, from Thy e-ter - nal throne
a tempo
p
p
Look with an eye of blessing down; While we pre - pare,
cresc.
with holy rites, To so-lemnize the Feast of Lights, the Feast of
p
cresc.
cresc.
Lights, to so - lem - nize the Feast of Lights.
cresc.
allargando
a tempo
cresc.
col canto
mf

The Messiah.
Isaiah vii., v. 14.-Matt. i., 23.
Recitative and Aria.
G. F. HÄNDEL.
Recit.
Be-hold! a vir-gin shall conceive, and bear a son,
and shall call his name Em - man - u - el: God with us.
Isaiah: xl, 9.–lx, 1.
Aria.
Andante. (♩.=54)

O thou that tell-est good ti-dings to Zi-on,
get thee up in-to the high moun- -tain!
O thou that tell-est good
ti-dings to Zi-on,
get thee

up in-to the high moun - - - - -
- - tain!
mf
get thee up in-to the high
f
cresc.
moun - - - - - - - -
(,)
- - - - tain!
tr
f

p
O thou that tell - est good ti - dings to Je - ru - sa - lem,
tr
p
p
p
f
lift up thy voice with
p
p
strength! lift it up, be not a - fraid!
cresc.
f
marcato
Say un - to the cit - ies of Ju - dah, say un - to the
cit - ies of Ju - dah: Be - hold your
cresc.
f
p
cresc.

God! be - hold your God! Say
p
cresc.
un - to the cit - ies of Ju - dah: Be - hold your
cresc.
f
God! be - hold your God!
p
f
be - hold your God!
f
p
O
f
p

mf
thou that tell-est good ti-dings to Zi-on, A-
tr
f
p
con spirito
rise, shine, for thy light is come;
p
f
A - rise, a - rise, a-
f
p
p
rise, shine, for thy light is come, And the glo-
p
mf
f
p
cresc.
-ry of the Lord, the
f
tr
f

glo - ry of the Lord is
con spirito
ris - en, is ris - en up - on thee, is ris - - en, is
ris - en up - on thee, the glo - ry, the
p
f
mf
glo - ry, the glo - ry of the Lord
allargando
is ris - en up - on thee.
colla voce

# The Messiah.

Isaiah: liii, 8-1. 6.

## Aria.

G. F. HÄNDEL.

grief.
a tempo
He
was despis-ed, re-ject-ed, He was des-pis-ed, and reject-ed of
men, a man of sorrows, and acquainted with grief, a man of sorrows, and ac-
quainted with grief. He was depis-ed, re-ject-ed, a man of
sorrows, and acquaint-ed with grief, and acquaint-ed with grief, a man of

più lento
sorrows, and ac - quaint - ed with grief.
p col canto
a tempo
f
p
Fine.
(♪ = 84) energico
mf
He gave His back to the smit - ers,
mp agitato
He gave His back to the smit - ers,
agitato
and His cheeks to
them that plucked off His hair, and His cheeks to

them that pluck-ed off His hair, and His cheeks to
them that plucked off His hair; He hid not His
cresc.
face from shame and spit-ting, He hid not His
cresc.
mf
p
face from shame, from shame,
dim.
p
cresc.
riten.
He hid not His face from shame, from shame and spitting.
cresc.
dim.



*D.C. al Fine.*

# Samson.

## Aria.*)

G. F. HÄNDEL.

*) When sung in its place in the Oratorio this Aria has no Da Capo. The Da Capo would of course be necessary, if sung as a detached Aria. *M. S.*

serv-ant in dis-tress!
Re-turn, O God! be-
fp
f
hold Thy serv-ant in dis-tress,
p
re-turn, O God, re-turn, O God of Hosts!
poco cresc.
poco riten.
a tempo
be-hold, be-hold, be-hold, be-hold Thy serv-ant, Thy
p col canto
f a tempo
p

servant in dis-tress,
be-hold, be-hold Thy
cresc.
servant, Thy servant in dis - tress!
cresc.
dim.
Re-turn, re-turn, O God, re-turn, O God of Hosts! be-hold, be-
p
ten.
allargando
hold Thy serv-ant in distress!
a tempo
ten.
col canto
f
tr
p
cresc.
Fine.

Poco più mosso.
mf
His might - y griefs, his might-y griefs re - dress. his might-y
mf
griefs, his might-y griefs, his might-y griefs re-dress,
cresc.
poco string.
Nor by the hea-then be they told, nor by the heathen be they told,
poco string.
His might-y griefs re - dress, Nor by the
più
cresc.
tranquilio
allargando
heathen, by the hea-then be they told, nor by the hea - then be they told.
allargando



D. C. al Fine

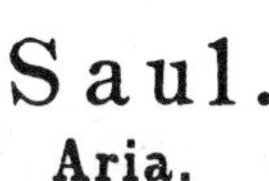


## Aria.

G. F. HÄNDEL.

Largo. (♩ = 66)

*p* *cresc.* *mp* *dim.* *p*

*p* *con espress.*

Oh Lord, whose mer - cies num-ber-less O'er all Thy works pre - vail, (o'er all Thy works, o'er all Thy works,)

*rall. a piacere* *a tempo*

o'er all Thy works pre - vail:

*col canto* *mp a tempo*

p
cresc.
Though dai - ly man Thy laws trans - gress,
mf
Thy patience cannot fail, no, cannot fail, Thy patience can - not
p
f
Lento molto
fail, (Thy pa - tience, Thy pa - tience,) Thy pa - tience cannot
fail.
mp
p Tempo I.
If yet his sins be not too
great, The bu - sy fiend con -

rall.
trol; the bus - y fiend con -
(the bus-y fiend, the bus-y fiend,)
rall.
trol;
p
Yet long - er for re -
mp
pent - ance wait,
p espress.
And heal his wounded soul, his wounded
mf
p
p
soul, and heal his wound - ed soul,
his wounded soul, his wounded
f molto lento
soul,
And heal his wounded soul.
f
molto lento
p
mp

# Solomon.

## Aria.

G. F. HÄNDEL.

ho - vah's power, How vain were all I_ knew! how vain,_ how
mp
vain_were all I_knew, how vain, how vain were all I
knew! What though I_
ten.
cresc.
p
trace each herb and_ flower, That drinks the morn - ing_
mp
con anima
dew, Did I not own Je-ho-vah's power, How
ten.
mf
p
p

mf
vain were all I knew! how vain were all I knew, how vain, how vain, how
vain were all I knew, how vain were all I knew!
ten.
p
mp
cresc.
f
mf un poco agitato cresc.
Say, what's the rest but emp - ty boast, The
Fine

più agitato e cresc.
pedant's i-dle claim, the pedant's i-dle claim, Who, having all the substance lost, At-
tempts to grasp a name? The ped-ant's i-dle claim,
p
the ped-ant's i-dle claim, Who, hav-ing all the
mf
cresc.
sub-stance lost, At-tempts to grasp a name, at-tempts to grasp a name?
f rall.
cresc.
rall.
D.C. al Fine.

# Susanna.

## Recitative and Aria.

G. F. HÄNDEL.

con tenerezza
first I saw my love-ly maid Be-neath the cit-ron's shade, In
cresc.
mf
na-tive in-no-cence array'd, My heart be-came her prize, my heart be-came her
p
cresc.
p
prize,
my heart became her prize;
mf
col canto
mf
p
When first I saw my love-ly maid Be-
p
p
neath the citron's shade, My heart be-came, my heart became her prize. When
cresc.
p

p
first I saw_my love_ly maid Be-neath the cit-ron's shade, In
mf
native in-no-cence array'd, My heart be-came, my heart became her prize, my_
p
mf
heart became her prize, my heart became, my heart became her prize, my
rall.
a tempo
heart be-came_her prize.
col canto
f a tempo

p p

I gaz'd, I lov'd, I gaz'd, I lov'd, I

*Fine*

p

mf

gaz'd __ a - gain, Could mor - tal breast from

mf

love __ re-frain? Her thou - sand vir - tues still main - tain The

p

con - - quest of __ her eyes; I gaz'd, _ I lov'd, _ I

*cresc.* *dim.* p

mf *poco allargando*

gaz'd ___ a - gain, Could mor - tal breast from love __ re-frain?

*col canto* f

*D. S. al Fine.*

# Theodora.

## Aria.

G. F. HÄNDEL.

cresc.
day we sing and pray, to Thee we pray, Lord, to
p
Thee, in hope we sing and pray,
cresc.
f
mf
to Thee each night and
p
day, to Thee we sing and pray,
p
p
mp
mf
Lord, to Thee, each night and day, Strong in hope we

mf
più lento
cresc.
sing___ and pray, we sing and pray, strong in hope___ we sing___ and
p
col canto
cresc.
pray.
mf a tempo
cresc.
f rall.
Fine
Allegro moderato. (♩ = 92)
f
Though con-vul-sive rocks the ground,
f
And Thy thunders roll a -
round,
f
and Thy thunders roll a - round,
p espress.
Still to Thee,
each night and
p

cresc.
day, still to Thee
mf
f
we sing and pray, though con-vul-sive rocks the
f
f
ground, and Thy thunders roll a - round,
p
cresc.
Adagio
still to Thee we sing and pray.
sf
p
Dal Segno al Fine.

# Christus.

## Arioso.

F. KIEL.

cresc.
fore _ her shear - ers. But thus saith God, _ the Lord: ___
cresc.
p
con solennità
___ I have for a small mo-ment thee _ for-sa-ken,
p
cresc.
but with great glo-ry and wor - - - ship will I
cresc.
f
f
crown ___ thee, will I crown _ thee. I
f
f

have al - so giv - en thee for a light to the Gen -
tiles, that thou may'st be my sal - va - -
cresc.
tion un - to the ends of the
poco sost.
poco sost.
earth, un - to the ends of the
p
earth.
Ped.

# The Star of Bethlehem.

Arioso.

Andante con moto. (♩ = 52)

F. KIEL.

come to ap - pear, to ap - pear be - fore the pres - ence of
poco f
God? Send forth Thy light and Thy truth,
p
that they may
lead me, may lead me and bring me un - to Thy ho - ly hill and to Thy
poco a poco cresc.
cresc.
pp
f
mf
mf
p
mf
dwell - ing, and that I may go in

p
to the al - tar of God,
p
ev'n to the
p
f
p
Ped.
cresc.
God of my joy,
dim.
of my joy and
cresc.
dim.
glad - - - ness, of my glad - - -
p
ness.
pp

# The Star of Bethlehem.

Arioso.

Andante. (♩ = 44) F. KIEL.

hast de - liv - er'd, hast de-liv-er'd my
pp
poco cresc.
soul from death, and mine eyes from tears, and my
poco cresc.
p
feet from fall - - - - - ing.
fz
p
dolce
Turn a - gain to thy rest, O my
cresc.
p

mf
soul,—
for the Lord— hath re-
cresc.
ward - - ed— thee, the Lord— hath—
—re - ward - ed thee, hath re - - ward - ed
thee.
p
pp
Ped.

# The Rose of Sharon.

**Aria.**

A. C. MACKENZIE.

plen - ti-ful field, gladness is ta-ken a-way, and
fz
joy out of the plen - ti-ful field; In the vine-yards there is no
p
mf
p
fz
mf
Ped.
Ped.
p
poco cresc.
sing - ing, in the vine-yards there is no sing - ing, nei-
p
poco cresc.
mf
mf
-ther is there an - y shout - ing, nei-ther is there an - y
mf

p
shout - ing, nei - ther is there an - y
p
p
rit.
a tempo
shout - - ing.
rit.
p a tempo
p
The tread - ers tread out no wine, no wine,
mf ad lib.
the tread - ers tread out no wine, no wine,
mf

p
no wine, And the noise of the vin - tage hath
p
mf
ceased, and the noise of the vin - tage hath ceased, hath ceased,
f
f
p
p
mf calando
hath ceased, and the noise of the vin - tage hath
p
calando
a tempo
p
p
ceased. Glad - ness is ta - ken a - way, is
Ped. *
mf
ta - ken, is ta - ken a - way, And joy out of the
cresc.

p
plen - ti-ful field;
In the vine-yard there is no
mf
mf
sing - ing,
nei-ther is there an - y shout - ing,
nei-ther is there an - y shout - ing,
nei-
- ther is there an-y shout - - ing.
rit.
rit.
cantabile

# The Miracle of Nain.

**Recitative and Aria.**

English version by
Dr. Th. Baker.

H. MARÉCHAL.

son af - ter the sire! The wid - ow all in tears, and the
moth - er de - spair - ful! Shall my woes nev-
a tempo
p
f
molto rit.
- er cease?
a tempo
ff
dim.
p
pp
Aria.
con espress.
p
One would

Andante.
say, he - re - pos - es, and that a smile yet
p
lin - gers, a ten - der smile yet faint - ly
colla voce
lin - gers in his eyes!
He is dead, the child I cher - ish!
Ye gods! how vain are all our mor - tal joys!

Ye gods! how vain are all our mor-tal joys!
cresc.
and how our ev-'ry hope is soon fled,
sf
oh, how our ev-'ry hope is soon fled!
p
dolce
In one day a-lone, ah me! can such a
poco cresc.
dolce e cantabile
poco cresc.
ten-der love be de-stroy'd, and all my hopes, all my
con ardore
f
sosten.
cresc.

hopes were nothing more than a dream, a
r.h.
f
dream that pass-es o-ver, leav-ing naught save a keen re-
Ped.
*
gret! Ah,
cresc.
stringendo
f
cresc.
con dolore
I have lost my son!
p
Ah!
sf
col canto
a tempo
cresc.
I have lost my son!
cresc.
sf
dim.

Tempo I.
suffocato
'Tis the end! all is o'er! Ah!
cresc.
p
dolce
cresc.
a piacere
'tis the end!
all is o'er!
f
dolce
Andante con moto.
sf molto espressivo
dim.
dim.

Elijah.
Aria.
Andantino. (♩ = 72)
F. MENDELSSOHN.
molto espress.
O rest in the Lord, wait pa-tient-ly for Him, and He shall
sempre pp
give thee thy heart's de - sires; O rest in the Lord, wait patient-ly for Him, and He shall
mf
give thee thy heart's de - sires, and He shall give thee thy heart's de-sires. Commit thy way un-
to Him, and trust in Him; commit thy way un-to Him, and trust in Him; and fret not thy-
cresc.
self — be-cause of e-vil-do-ers. O rest in the Lord, wait pa-tient-ly for

poco rall.
a tempo
Him, wait pa-tient-ly for Him; O rest in the Lord; wait pa-tient-ly for
pp
rall.
a tempo
cresc.
f
Him, and He shall give thee thy heart's de-sires, and He shall
cresc.
sf
f
dim.
give thee thy heart's de - sires, and He shall give thee thy heart's de-
p
sf
p
p
cresc.
sires. O rest in the Lord, O rest in the Lord, and wait,
pp
cresc.
p
wait pa-tient-ly for Him.
pp
Ped.

# St. Paul.

## Recitative and Arioso.

Acts ix: 2.

F. MENDELSSOHN.

p
ritard.
a tempo
dren. But the Lord is mind-ful of His own, the
ritard.
a tempo
cresc.
Lord re-mem-bers His chil - dren, re- mem - - bers His
cresc.
chil - dren.
p
mf
p
Bow down be-fore Him, ye might - y,
mf
cresc.
for the Lord is
p
fp
cresc.
near us,
p
bow down be-fore Him, ye might - y,
f
p
fp

mf
cresc.
f
p
for the Lord is near us. Yea, the
cresc.
f
dim.
p
Lord is mind-ful of His own, He re - mem-bers His chil - -
dren. Bow down be - fore Him, ye might - y, for the
cresc.
f
Lord is near us.
dim.
pp

# Judith.

## Aria.

C. H. H. PARRY.

15891

all our sins.
Animando
Animando
Even now, unto your mourning city
Allegro sostenuto.
He bringeth home your King.
tranquillo
un poco agitato
No more the voice of the oppressor shall ye fear,
No more a shameful tribute shall ye pay,

*f con spirito* *cresc.*

The Lord Him-self will fight for you, His arm shall o-ver-throw your

*cresc.*

*cresc.*

en-e-mies; And Je-ru - sa - lem ___ from her stain shall be

*tr*

*cresc.*

cleans-ed and shine as a bride, and shine as a

*cresc.*

*rit.* *a tempo*

bride in the morn - - ing of her bri-dal.

*a tempo*

*rit.* *mf*

*Allegretto semplice.*

*p*

Your streets a-gain shall ech-o with your chil - drens

*poco rit.* *p a tempo*

cresc.
voic - es, your folds shall be full a-gain with your bleat - ing flocks, your
fields shall al - so stand so thick with rip-en-ing corn that they shall
laugh, that they shall laugh and
sing.
rit. molto
col canto
Lento.
The Lord is long - suf - fer - ing and mer - ci - ful,

He keep-eth not His an-ger for ev-er.
p
p
He look-ed on our af-flic-tion and
p
pain,
f
And hath for-giv-en us,
mf
and hath for-giv-en us
molto rall.
all our
p
col canto
sins.
a tempo
pp

# The World's End.

Recitative and Aria.

J. RAFF.

with thy sharp sick-le,
and ga-ther the clusters of the
f
p
f
p
vine,
her grapes are full, full and
ripe.
rit.
Aria.
Adagio. (♩= 96)
p f p
mf
Great
and won-der-ful are
all Thy works,
Lord!
p f p

p
mf
And just and true, O Lord, all Thy ways, Thou King of the
Ho-ly! Thou King of the Ho-ly! Thou King of the
f
Ho-ly!
mf
Who shall not fear thee, Lord,
p
cresc.
and glo-ri-fy Thy ho-ly Name?
f
for Thou a-lone art
ho-ly, for Thou a-lone art ho-ly!
Great

p mf
— and won-der-ful are all Thy works,

f p mf
Lord! And just and true are all Thy ways, Thou

f f
King of the Ho-ly! Thou King of the Ho-ly! Thou King of the

p f p f pesante
Ho-ly! Lord! Thou a-lone art ho-

ly!

# The World's End.

**Aria.**

J. RAFF.

tears from their eyes,
God shall
wipe a-way all
tears from their
eyes.
And
death is no more, nor sor - row, nor
cry - ing, and pain shall be no more,

and pain shall be no more, for the
former things have passed away, the former, the
first things have passed away.
Behold, the House of God is with
men. And He will dwell with them, and

they shall be His peo - ple, and He will dwell

with them, and they shall be His peo - - ple,

they shall be His peo - - ple,

they shall be His peo - - ple.

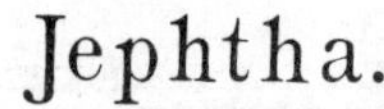


**Cavatina.**

C. RHEINTHALER.

Larghetto.

*pp e legato*

*p con espressione*

The Lord will not be ev - er wroth, the Lord will not be ev - er wroth,

*p* *mf*

*p* *cresc.*

but with mer-cy un - end-ing, with mer-cy un - end-ing a - gain, —

*pp* *cresc.*

— a - gain ——— will spare us!

*mf*

*mf*

The Lord will not be ev - er wroth.

*p*

If ye will

*p* *p*

cresc.
seek Him with all your hearts, if ye will seek Him with all your
cresc.
hearts, then shall ye sure-ly find Him, then shall ye sure-ly find Him, then shall ye
cresc.
p
sure-ly find Him; if ye will seek Him with all your
p
cresc.
hearts, if ye will seek Him with all your hearts, then shall ye
poco rit.
a tempo
surely find Him; then shall ye sure-ly find Him.
rit.
a tempo

# Christmas Oratorio.

## Aria.

C. SAINT-SAËNS.

p
have I wait - ed for the
Lord, have I wait - - ed, have
I wait - ed for the Lord.
And
cresc.
dim.
espressivo
dolce
pp

cresc.
lo! — he heard my cry, and lo! — he
cresc.
cresc.
heard my cry, and — lo! he heard, and lo! — he
dim.
Ped.
sempre Ped.
mf
heard, and — lo! — he heard, —
sf
and lo! he heard — my cry.

# "The Heavens declare."

**Arioso.**

C. SAINT-SAËNS.

più cresc.
deem-er, Thou O Lord, art my Pro - tect - or, and my Re -
più cresc.
deem-er, and my Re - deem - er,
dolce
Thou, O Lord,
dolce
art my Pro - tect - or, art my Pro - tect - or, and
cresc.
Thou my Re-deem-er, Thou art my Pro-tect-or,
mf
p
mf
cresc.
dim.
Thou art my Re - deem-er, Thou, O
p

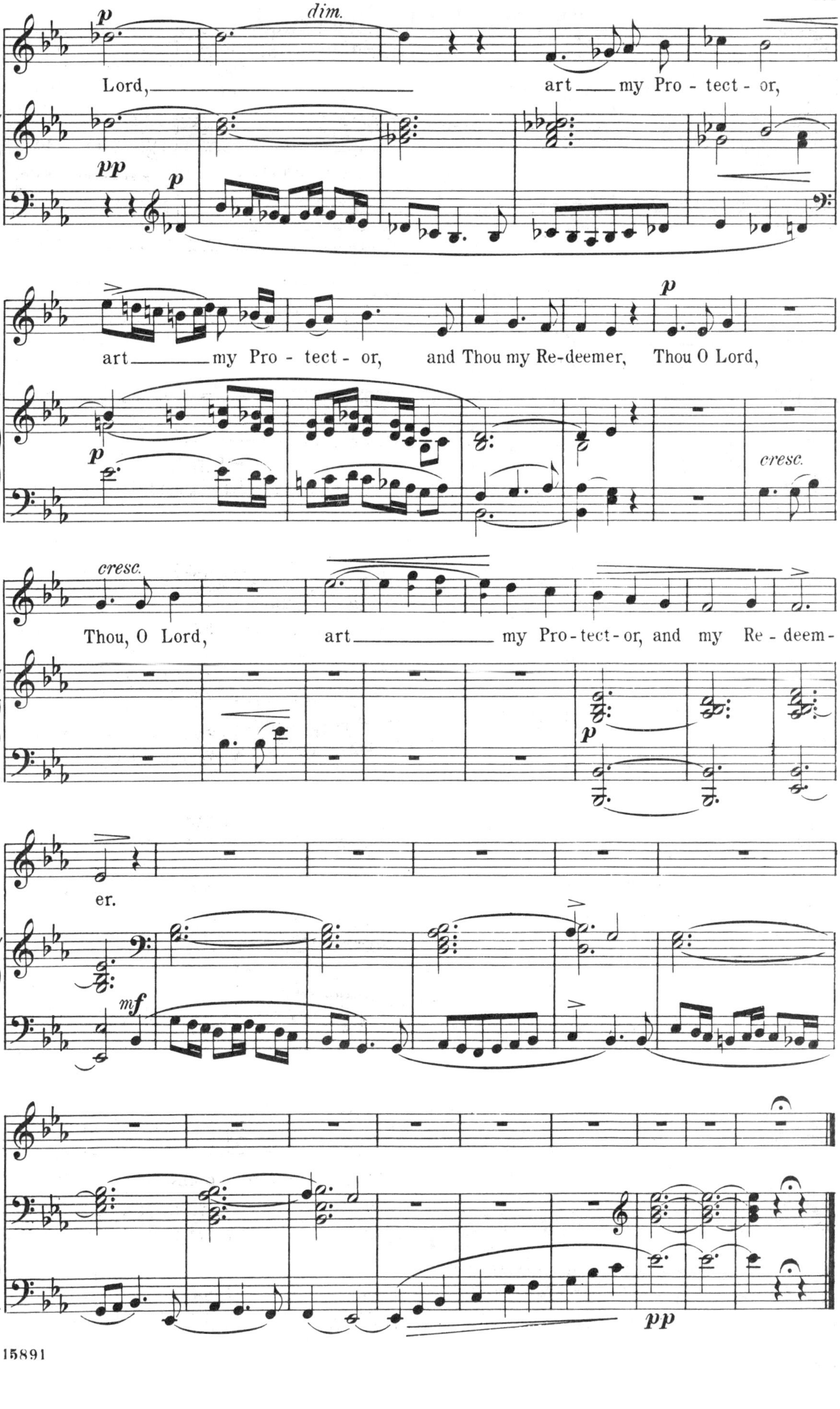

p
dim.
Lord, art my Pro - tect - or,
pp
p
art my Pro - tect - or, and Thou my Re-deemer, Thou O Lord,
p
cresc.
cresc.
Thou, O Lord, art my Pro - tect - or, and my Re - deem -
p
er.
mf
pp

# The Light of the World.

**Aria.**

Andante moderato. (♩ = 88)

Sir A. SULLIVAN.

p
God shall wipe a-way all tears from their eyes, There shall be
p
poco cresc.
no more death, nei-ther sor - row nor cry - ing,
f
nei - ther shall there be any more pain, For the
poco cresc.
meno f
for-mer things are pass'd a - way. Be - hold, I make
f
meno f
p
f
all things new, saith the Lord, For the for-mer things are
p
f

f
pass'd a - way. Be - hold, I make all things
meno f
dim.
rall.
new, saith the Lord, saith the Lord.
dim.
p
rall.
p a tempo
God shall wipe a - way all tears from their eyes, There shall be
pp
cresc.
no more death, nei - ther sor - row nor cry - ing,
cresc.
nei - ther shall there be any more pain, and

*f*

God shall wipe a - way all tears, all tears from their eyes.

*dim.*

*p*

There shall be no more death, nei - ther sor - row nor cry - ing,

*con abbandono* *rall.*

nei - ther sor - row nor cry - ing

*cresc.* *rall.* *p* *colla voce*

Ped. *

# The Prodigal Son.

## Aria.

Sir A. SULLIVAN.

cresc.
world, for the world pass - eth a - way, for the world pass - eth a -
cresc.
f
dim.
way, the world pass - eth a - way, and the lust there -
f
sf
dim.
p
cresc.
of. But he that do - eth the will of
p
cresc.
f
God, a - bid - eth for ev - - er,
f

dim.
a - bid - eth for ev - er.
dim.
p
Ped.
p
He that do - eth the will of
p
poco cresc.
dim. e rall.
God, a - bid - eth for ev - - er.
dim.
rall.
con sentimento
p
Love not the world, nor the things that are in the world, for the
p

cresc.
f
world pass-eth a - way, and the lust there - of. But he that
cresc.
sf
f
dim.
do - eth the will of God, a - bid - eth for ev - er, a -
dim.
pp
bid - eth, a - bid - eth for ev - er,
poco cresc.
pp
p tranquillo
a - bid - eth for ev - er.
pp
Ped. * Ped.

# Constantin.

**Recitative and Aria.**

English version by
Dr. Th. Baker.

G. VIERLING.

round. Be si - lent, ye ech - oes of earth - ly de - sire! Here
sempre più tranquillo
still-ness is reign-ing, Here rest-ful-ness on - ly my heart shall in - spire.
p dolce
Aria.
Andante con moto.
Lord, Lord, for whom my soul is burn - ing,
Ten - - der Sav - iour,

ten - der Sav - iour, all my yearn - ing,
all my yearn - ing Thine shall be for ev - er - more,
for ev - er, for ev - er, ev - er-
more! See, the world would
fain mis-lead me, Who the roy - al band do wear,
cresc.

mf
p
Still with ar - dent vows of pas - sion Plead-ing, plead-ing, fain my heart would
snare. Lord, Lord, Let my faith be nev-er
sha - ken! Lord, Thou who a - lone art
f
cresc.
light, Lord, drive a - way this sin - ful
yearn - ing; Lord, to whom my soul is turn - ing, Drive a -

f
way this sin-ful yearn - ing, Strength - en me, for-sake me
f poco espress.
not, strength - en me, for - sake me
cresc.
f
dim.
dim.
mf
not, strength - en me,
p
pp
f
p
mf
con abbandono
strength - en me, for-sake me not!
mf dolce
mf
f
mf dolce
pp
pp

# Gethsemane.

**Aria.**

Un poco più mosso.
mf
As Thou wilt, Fa - ther, though my way Be lone - ly, dark and
drear; As Thou wilt, when no heav'nly ray Comes through the dark to
cheer,— But aw - ful shapes and sounds af - fright, Like
accel.
accel.
cresc.
dread - ful vis-ions of the night, like
cresc.
f
f
dread - ful vis-ions of the night.
Adagio.
mf
pp

Andante.

*p*

O gracious Father, wise and kind, Thou knowest what is best,

*pp*

And oft through storms Thy children find The haven of Thy rest, the haven of Thy rest.

*p*

Lord, grant me, when earth's troubles cease,

*pp*

Adagio.

*pp*

To enter Thine eternal peace.

*pp colla voce*

*mf*

A - - - men.